# Contents

## Learn the Drums for Kids: Book 1

# Welcome

## Welcome to Learn the drums for Kids, Book 1
## written by Sean Palmer

Sean is a drum tutor who has taught children how to play the Drums professionally in primary, secondary and grammar schools, Special Educational Needs schools, music schools and also online since 2005.

Seans teaches with a fun and enjoyable approach. He says if his students are having fun, then they are learning and will develop their musical skills at a much faster pace.

Sean has taught thousands of students how to achieve their goals as drummers since he started teaching back in May 2005!

## About this book

Learn the drums for Kids book 1 is for the absolute beginner drummer looking to learn how to play the drums. This book teaches you not only how to play the drums but also how to read drum music in the most fun and enjoyable way possible using Sean's extremely successful match and play colour note system. This book is designed for you to work through over a period of 7 days and will give you a great introduction to the drums. In this book you'll learn how to play a variety of different drum grooves and fills.

# About the Match and Play colour note system

Learning how to play the drums has always been fun, but let's face it, learning how to read sheet music can be off putting, boring, time consuming and can sometimes feel like an impossible task.

The match and play colour note system within this book changes this by turning the process of reading music into a fun and enjoyable game-like activity.

This book comes with colour attachments that you'll place on each part of your drum kit. You'll then simply match and play the colour notes on the sheet music in this book with the same colour attachment on your drums. That is it, you're away reading music and playing the drums!

## How it works:

If a colour note on the sheet music is by itself, then just hit that one part of your drum kit alone, if there are multiple colour notes stacked on top of each other, then simply play these parts of your kit together at the same time as seen below in these examples.

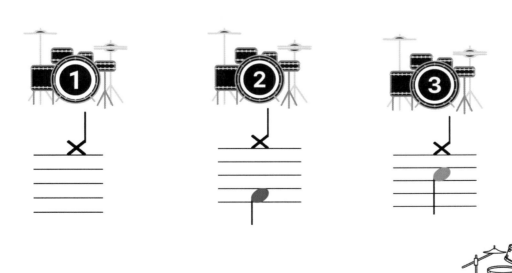

# Day 1
## Parts of the Drum kit

# The Attachments

Simply cut and attach these attachments to the correct part of your drums kit.

Use page 3 to help you put the correct attachment onto the correct drum.

I would suggest using sticky tape to attach these to your drums.

Always use an adults supervision when using scissors

---

## Bass drum

## Hi-hat

# Snare drum

# Tom 1

# Tom 2

# Tom 3

6

# How to sit at the drum kit

To sit at the drum kit correctly, sit facing your drum kit with your left foot flat on the Hi-hat pedal, put your right foot on the bass drum pedal making sure you keep your back straight.

# How to hold the drum sticks

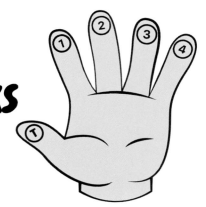

It is important to hold your drum sticks correctly. To do this, for each hand, hold the bottom of the drum stick with your thumb and finger 1. Wrap the remaining fingers (2, 3 and 4) around your drum stick. Make sure you don't squeeze the drum stick to tight. Try this with both hands.

# How to hit
# the drums

We're going to use the Snare drum to practice this on.

1) Position the drum stick slightly above the centre of the snare drum with the tip (top) of the drumstick in the middle.

2) Raise your drum stick slightly using your wrist.

3) Strike the snare drum with the tip (top) of your drum stick using all motion from your wrist.

4) Raise the stick back up to the starting position.

That is how to hit a drum. This can be used to hit all parts of your drum kit apart from the bass drum.

# How to hit the Bass drum

To hit the bass drum correctly, place your right foot on the bass drum pedal. Lift up the heel of your foot slightly and then raise up you knee just a bit, the beater of you bass drum pedal should move away from the bass drum when you do this. Next, push your foot back down. At this point the beater on the bass drum pedal should strike the bass drum, Try not to lift your knee too high. The front of your foot should remain on the pedal at all times.

# The musical symbols

Throughout this book you will see some odd symbols that might confuse you, if you would like to know what they mean, have a read below.

This is known as a Percussion Cleff. It tells you this music is written for drummers.

This is a 4 beat rest . A rest is not played.

This is known as a Time Signature. It tells you how many beats are in each bar.

This is a 1 beat rest. A rest is not played.

This is known as a Stave or Staff. It tells you what part of the drum kit is to be played, depending what line the note is on.

This is a Bar Marker. It marks out the end of one bar and the beginning of the next.

# Understanding the Quarter note

The note above is called a Quarter note or a Crotchet.

A Quarter note has a value of one beat.

To count one Quarter note you just need to count " 1 ".

It is important to count your note's correctly when playing them on your drum kit.

To count 4 Quarter notes correctly as seen below, you must count " 1 2 3 4 " The numbers are referring to the beats.

Have a go at playing 4 Quarter notes on the Snare drum with your right drum stick.

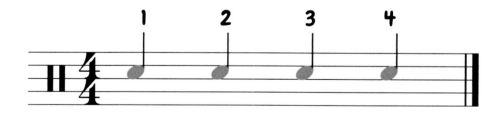

# Understanding the Eighth note

The note above is called an Eighth note or a Quaver.

An Eighth note has a value of half of a beat.

Due to this, you will need 2 Eighth notes as shown below to make one whole beat.

To count one beat of Eighth notes you need to count " 1 & ".

It is important to count your note's correctly when playing them on your drum kit.

To count 4 beats of Eighth notes correctly as seen below, you must count " 1 & 2 & 3 & 4 & "

Have a go at playing 8 Eighth notes on the Snare drum alternating between the drum sticks in your right and left hand. If this was played on the Hi-hat, you would only use the drum stick in your right hand.

# Day 2
# Explained

To check what you are playing sounds correct, have a listen to the audio tracks associated with this book. To access the tracks, go to www.bandskills.com

### On line 1
Hit the Hi-hat 4 times with the drum stick in your right hand.

### On line 2
Play the same thing again, but for 4 times through.

### On line 3
Whilst still hitting the Hi-hat, hit the Snare drum on beat 2 and beat 4 with the drum stick in your left hand. Make sure your right arm is above your left arm.

### On line 4
Play the same thing again, but for 4 times through.

### On line 5
Whilst still hitting the Hi-hat and Snare drum, add in the Bass drum on beats 1 and 3 with your right foot.

### On line 6
Play the same thing again, but for 4 times.

### On line 7
Using only the drum stick in the right hand, hit the Snare drum then Tom 1 then Tom 2 and then Tom 3 once per drum.

### On line 8
Play the same thing again, but for 4 times through.

### On line 9
Now it's time to put together what you have learnt in today's lesson. I recommend working through this until you're satisfied with how it sounds.

# Day 2

By Sean Palmer

# Day 3 Explained

To check what you are playing sounds correct, have a listen to the audio tracks associated with this book. To access the tracks, go to
www.bandskills.com

### On line 1
Hit the Hi-hat with the drum stick in the right hand 8 times. You're playing Eighth notes here so the correct way to count this is 1 & 2 & 3 & 4 & .

### On line 2
Play exactly the same thing again but for 4 times.

### On Line 3
Add in the Snare drum with the left drum stick on beats 2 and 4

### On line 4
Play exactly the same thing again but for 4 times through.

### On line 5
Whilst still hitting the Hi-hat and Snare drum, add in the Bass drum on beats 1 and 3 with your right foot.

### On line 6
Play the same thing again, but for 4 times through.

### On line 7
Hit the Snare drum with the right and then left drum stick, do the same on Tom 1, Tom 2 and then Tom 3.

### On line 8
Play the same thing again, but for 4 times through.

### On line 9
Now it's time to put together what you have learnt in today's lesson. I recommend working through this until you're satisfied with how it sounds.

# Day 3

# Day 4 Explained

To check what you are playing sounds correct, have a listen to the audio tracks associated with this book. To access the tracks, go to www.bandskills.com

Lines 1 - 4 are exactly the same as the previous lesson, still go through these as a warm up to prepare you for line 5.

## On line 5
Whilst still hitting the Hi-hat and Snare drum, add in the Bass drum on beats 1 and on beats 3 and the & of beats 3 with your right foot.

## On line 6
Play the same thing again, but for 4 times.

## On line 7
Hit the Snare drum with your right drum stick, then Tom 1 with your right and then your left drum stick, hit Tom 2 with your right drum stick and then Tom 3 with your right and then your left drum stick.

## On line 8
Play the same thing again, but for 4 times.

## On line 9
Now it's time to put together what you have learnt in today's lesson. I recommend working through this until you're satisfied with how it sounds.

# Day 4

By Sean Palmer

20

# Day 5 Explained

To check what you are playing sounds correct, have a listen to the audio tracks associated with this book. To access the tracks, go to www.bandskills.com

Lines 1 - 4 are exactly the same as the previous lesson, still go through these as a warm up to prepare you for line 5.

## On line 5
Whilst still playing the Hi-hat and Snare drum, add in the Bass drum on the 1 and the & of beats 1 and then the 3 and the & of beats 3.

## On line 6
Play the same thing again, but for 4 times.

## On line 7
Hit the Snare drum once with the right drum stick, then Tom 1 with the right and then left drum stick, Tom 2 with the right and then left drum stick and then Tom 3 with the right and then left drum stick.

## On line 8
Play the same thing again, but for 4 times.

## On line 9
Now it's time to put together what you have learnt in today's lesson. I recommend working through this until you're satisfied with how it sounds.

# Day 5

By Sean Palmer

# Day 6
# Explained

To check what you are playing sounds correct, have a listen to the audio tracks associated with this book. To access the tracks, go to
www.bandskills.com

Lines 1 - 4 are exactly the same as the previous lesson, still go through these as a warm up to prepare you for line 5.

### On line 5
Whilst still playing the Hi-hat and Snare drum, add in the Bass drum on the 1 and the & of Beats 1, and then on beats 3.

### On line 6
Play the same thing again, but for 4 times.

### On line 7
Hit the Snare drum with the right drum stick, then Tom 1 with the right and then left drum stick, then hit Tom 2 with the right and then left drum stick and then Tom 3 with the right drum stick.

### On line 8
Play the same thing again, but for 4 times.

### On line 9
Now it's time to put together what you have learnt in today's lesson. I recommend working through this until you're satisfied with how it sounds.

# Day 6

By Sean Palmer

# Day 7
# Explained

To check what you are playing sounds correct, have a listen to the audio tracks associated with this book. To access the tracks, go to www.bandskills.com

Lines 1 - 4 are exactly the same as the previous lesson, still go through these as a warm up to prepare you for line 5.

### On line 5
Whilst still playing the Hi-hat and Snare drum, add in the Bass drum on Beats 1, 2 ,3 and 4.

### On line 6
Play the same thing again, but for 4 times.

### On line 7
Hit the Snare drum with the right and then left drum stick, Tom 1 with the right and then left drum stick, Tom 2 with the right drum stick and then Tom 3 with the right drum stick.

### On line 8
Play the same thing again, but for 4 times.

### On line 9
Now it's time to put together what you have learnt in today's lesson. I recommend working through this until you're satisfied with how it sounds.

### Complete!
Congratulations, you've now completed this book! don't forget to check out the next book in this series!

# Day 7

By Sean Palmer

26

Made in the USA
Middletown, DE
13 October 2023

40748167R00015